**NATURE'S GROSSEST**

# CHICKS EAT PUKE!

By Bert Wilberforce

**Gareth Stevens**
PUBLISHING

Please visit our website, www.garethstevens.com. For a free color catalog of all our high-quality books, call toll free 1-800-542-2595 or fax 1-877-542-2596.

Cataloging-in-Publication Data

Names: Wilberforce, Bert.
Title: Chicks eat puke! / Bert Wilberforce.
Description: New York : Gareth Stevens Publishing, 2018. | Series: Nature's grossest | Includes index.
Identifiers: ISBN 9781538209417 (pbk.) | ISBN 9781538209431 (library bound) | ISBN 9781538209424 (6 pack)
Subjects: LCSH: Birds–Infancy–Juvenile literature.
Classification: LCC QL676.2 W57 2018 | DDC 598.13'92–dc23

Published in 2018 by
**Gareth Stevens Publishing**
111 East 14th Street, Suite 349
New York, NY 10003

Copyright © 2018 Gareth Stevens Publishing

Designer: Laura Bowen
Editor: Therese Shea

Photo credits: Cover, p. 1 Louise Murray/age fotostock/Getty Images; pp. 3–24 (background) Oleksii Natykach/Shutterstock.com; p. 5 Soru Epotok/Shutterstock.com; p. 7 Anneka/Shutterstock.com; p. 9 Federico Massa/Shutterstock.com; p. 11 Dikky Oesin/Shutterstock.com; p. 13 Education Images/Universal Images Group/Getty Images; p. 15 sirtravelalot/Shutterstock.com; p. 17 Jim Brandenburg/Minden Pictures/Getty Images; p. 19 B Norris/Shutterstock.com; p. 21 PCHT/Shutterstock.com.

All rights reserved. No part of this book may be reproduced in any form without permission in writing from the publisher, except by a reviewer.

Printed in the United States of America

CPSIA compliance information: Batch #CW18GS: For further information contact Gareth Stevens, New York, New York at 1-800-542-2595.

# CONTENTS

Chick Chow . . . . . . . . . . . . . . . . . . . . . . . 4

Nest Life . . . . . . . . . . . . . . . . . . . . . . . . . 6

Family Food . . . . . . . . . . . . . . . . . . . . . 10

Variety of Vomit . . . . . . . . . . . . . . . . . . 18

Still Grossed Out? . . . . . . . . . . . . . . . . 20

Glossary . . . . . . . . . . . . . . . . . . . . . . . 22

For More Information . . . . . . . . . . . . . 23

Index . . . . . . . . . . . . . . . . . . . . . . . . . 24

**Boldface** words appear in the glossary.

# Chick Chow

Think of the grossest food you've eaten. Did you have to eat it because it was good for you? Chicks eat something much grosser than anything you've tried. They eat their parents' puke, or throw up! And it's good for them!

5

## Nest Life

Most baby birds are called chicks. When chicks first **hatch** from their egg, they're called hatchlings. Hatchlings often have few feathers. That's why one of their parents sits on the nest to keep them warm.

7

Hatchlings stay in the nest while they grow feathers. The birds grow fast, so they need a lot of food. How do they get food in the nest? They count on their parents to bring food to them. Sometimes, the parents have already eaten this food!

9

# Family Food

Birds that eat seeds or berries can throw them up for chicks. Other birds travel long **distances** to find food such as fish. Another animal might steal the food on the way back. The bird eats the food to keep it safe!

11

Seabirds such as herring gulls feed their chicks food they've already eaten. First, a herring gull chick pecks on the red spot on its parent's **beak**. Then, the parent regurgitates, or throws up, some food for it!

13

Regurgitated food is partly broken down in a bird's stomach. This makes it easier for chicks to eat and break it down more in their own body. Emperor penguins feed fish to their young in this way.

15

Pelicans eat and throw up fish. They also eat **shellfish** and even other kinds of birds! They bring these regurgitated foods to their chicks, too. When chicks are old enough, pelican parents start feeding them whole foods.

17

## Variety of Vomit

Birds throw up food for other reasons, too. A bird that stays on its nest can't get food. Its **mate** might regurgitate to feed it. A bird looking for a mate may throw up to show it can care for a family!

19

# Still Grossed Out?

Now that you know more about it, is bird puke still gross to you? It's a common **behavior** that keeps chicks healthy. When someone tells you to eat your vegetables, remember it's not as bad as a chick's food!

21

# GLOSSARY

**beak:** the hard, usually pointed parts that cover a bird's mouth

**behavior:** the way an animal acts, or behaves

**distance:** the amount of space between two places or things

**hatch:** to break out

**mate:** one of two animals that come together to make babies

**shellfish:** an animal such as a crab or an oyster that has a hard outer shell and that lives in water

# FOR MORE INFORMATION

## BOOKS

Coleman, Miriam. *Skua Seabirds Eat Vomit!* New York, NY: PowerKids Press, 2014.

Kennington, Tammy. *Penguins.* Ann Arbor, MI: Cherry Lake Publishing, 2014.

Rustad, Martha E. H. *Do Chicks Ask for Snacks? Noticing Animal Behaviors.* Minneapolis, MN: Millbrook Press, 2016.

## WEBSITES

**Birds**
*kids.nationalgeographic.com/animals/hubs/birds/*
Find out about your favorite birds here.

**The Life of Birds: Parenthood**
*www.pbs.org/lifeofbirds/home/*
Read how many kinds of birds care for their young.

**Publisher's note to educators and parents:** Our editors have carefully reviewed these websites to ensure that they are suitable for students. Many websites change frequently, however, and we cannot guarantee that a site's future contents will continue to meet our high standards of quality and educational value. Be advised that students should be closely supervised whenever they access the Internet.

# INDEX

berries  10

eggs  6

emperor penguins  14

fish  10, 14, 16

food  4, 8, 10, 12, 14, 16, 18, 20

hatchlings  6, 8

herring gulls  12

mate  18

nest  6, 8, 18

parents  4, 6, 8, 12, 16

pelicans  16

puke  4, 20

seabirds  12

seeds  10

stomach  14